Recognise your achievements while navigating your way through learning with Dyslexia.

Copy Right © 2019 Emily Thuysbaert

Copy right © Emily Thuysbaert 2019

All rights reserved. No part of this publication may be reproduced, distributed or transmitted in any form or by any means, including photocopying, recording, or other electrical or mechanical methods, without prior written permission of the Author.

Illustrations by Luna Plum
Book Design by Mia Publications

If you would like to contact Emily Thuysbaert about her dyslexia awareness projects you can by email:

emilythuysbaert@yahoo.co.uk

© Emily Thuysbaert 2019

Introduction

Being a dyslexic myself I know all to well, the feeling of under achieving. I would always hear about what I was doing wrong or that I was not applying myself fully.
There was no focus on the good things I accomplished. So I remember my period of learning as being a very difficult time for me.

The aim of the **Dyslexic Writing Journal** is to help dyslexics see a pathway to success, to increase self esteem and to believe anything is possible.

I have put weekly inspirational quotes throughout this Journal to inspire you to **Dream Big Dreams**.

I want you to use this journal to help you set manageable goals and to look back over the weeks to see what you have achieved, no matter how small you think they were.

All great things take time to grow!!

How to use your amazing Journal

Start by writing / drawing how you feel before you do any writing.

I always found it difficult to organise and express my thoughts and ideas into the written form.

Being a visual dyslexic I use images to help prompt my writing.

Feelings – more often than not we will see writing as another thing that challenges us. It might be because we don't know how to spell something or what a word means so we shy away from the act of writing.

I want you to fall in love with writing so write about anything that interests you or that makes you happy.

Goals – Think what your overall goal for writing would be.

Mine was to be able to write a meaningful story and that it would actually make sense to people.

Think about what you could do bit by bit to make that goal become a reality, once you think you have mastered that writing goal, write a new goal down.

Review – Make sure you write down what you did because it is the key to your success.
It will allow you to see what is working and what isn't and can help minimise the feelings of frustration.

Remember – I just want you, to want to write about anything that interests you and knowing you don't have to have anyone mark it or correct it. The writing journal can be your secret journal.

Last of all – Dream Big Dreams

Please email me and let me know your weekly progress.

Because I know you are amazing I want to award you with a weekly writing certificate.

It's not just any writing certificate it's a magic certificate to praise you and your magic brain!!

Emily x

When you know BETTER you do BETTER

– Maya Angelou

Date:

Before writing I was feeling_____

When writing, how do I want to feel?
1._____
2._____
3._____

What is my goal today for writing?
_____
_____

What did I do today to achieve my goal?
_____
_____

Writing Review Time: What worked and didn't work for me today?
_____
_____

★ DREAM BIG DREAMS ★

Date:

Before writing I was feeling_____

When writing, how do I want to feel?
1._____
2._____
3._____

What is my goal today for writing?
_____
_____

What did I do today to achieve my goal?
_____
_____

Writing Review Time: What worked and didn't work for me today?
_____
_____

★ DREAM BIG DREAMS ★

Date:

Before writing I was feeling _____

When writing, how do I want to feel?
1._____
2._____
3._____

What is my goal today for writing?
_____
_____

What did I do today to achieve my goal?
_____
_____

Writing Review Time: What worked and didn't work for me today?
_____
_____

★ DREAM BIG DREAMS ★

Date:

Before writing I was feeling _____

When writing, how do I want to feel?
1._____
2._____
3._____

What is my goal today for writing?
_____
_____

What did I do today to achieve my goal?
_____
_____

Writing Review Time: What worked and didn't work for me today?
_____
_____

★ DREAM BIG DREAMS ★

Date:

Before I writing I was feeling_____

When writing, how do I want to feel?
1._____
2._____
3._____

What is my goal today for writing?
_____
_____

What did I do today to achieve my goal?
_____
_____

Writing Review Time: What worked and didn't work for me today?
_____
_____

★ DREAM BIG DREAMS ★

> Tell me and I forget, teach me and I may remember, involve me and I learn.
>
> —Benjamin Franklin

Date:

Before writing I was feeling_____

When writing, how do I want to feel?
1._____
2._____
3._____

What is my goal today for writing?
_____
_____

What did I do today to achieve my goal?
_____
_____

Writing Review Time: What worked and didn't work for me today?
_____
_____

★ DREAM BIG DREAMS ★

Date:

Before writing I was feeling_____

When writing, how do I want to feel?
1._____
2._____
3._____

What is my goal today for writing?
_____
_____

What did I do today to achieve my goal?
_____
_____

Writing Review Time: What worked and didn't work for me today?
_____
_____

★ DREAM BIG DREAMS ★

Date:

Before writing I was feeling_____

When writing, how do I want to feel?
1._____
2._____
3._____

What is my goal today for writing?
_____
_____

What did I do today to achieve my goal?
_____
_____

Writing Review Time: What worked and didn't work for me today?
_____
_____

★ DREAM BIG DREAMS ★

Date:

Before writing I was feeling_____

When writing, how do I want to feel?
1._____
2._____
3._____

What is my goal today for writing?
_____
_____

What did I do today to achieve my goal?
_____
_____

Writing Review Time: What worked and didn't work for me today?
_____
_____

★ DREAM BIG DREAMS ★

Date:

Before writing I was feeling_____

When writing, how do I want to feel?
1._____
2._____
3._____

What is my goal today for writing?
_____
_____

What did I do today to achieve my goal?
_____
_____

Writing Review Time: What worked and didn't work for me today?
_____
_____

★ DREAM BIG DREAMS ★

Date:

Before writing I was feeling_____

When writing, how do I want to feel?
1._____
2._____
3._____

What is my goal today for writing?
_____
_____

What did I do today to achieve my goal?
_____
_____

Writing Review Time: What worked and didn't work for me today?
_____
_____

★ DREAM BIG DREAMS ★

Date:

Before writing I was feeling_____

When writing, how do I want to feel?
1._____
2._____
3._____

What is my goal today for writing?
_____
_____

What did I do today to achieve my goal?
_____
_____

Writing Review Time: What worked and didn't work for me today?
_____
_____

★ DREAM BIG DREAMS ★

Education is not the filling of a pail, but the lighting of a fire.
― W.B Yeats

Date:

Before writing I was feeling_____

When writing, how do I want to feel?
1._____
2._____
3._____

What is my goal today for writing?
_____
_____

What did I do today to achieve my goal?
_____
_____

Writing Review Time: What worked and didn't work for me today?
_____
_____

★ DREAM BIG DREAMS ★

Date:

Before writing I was feeling_____

When writing, how do I want to feel?
1._____
2._____
3._____

What is my goal today for writing?
_____
_____

What did I do today to achieve my goal?
_____
_____

Writing Review Time: What worked and didn't work for me today?
_____
_____

★ DREAM BIG DREAMS ★

Date:

Before writing I was feeling_____

When writing, how do I want to feel?
1._____
2._____
3._____

What is my goal today for writing?
_____
_____

What did I do today to achieve my goal?
_____
_____

Writing Review Time: What worked and didn't work for me today?
_____
_____

★ DREAM BIG DREAMS ★

Date:

Before writing I was feeling_____

When writing, how do I want to feel?
1._____
2._____
3._____

What is my goal today for writing?
_____
_____

What did I do today to achieve my goal?
_____
_____

Writing Review Time: What worked and didn't work for me today?
_____
_____

★ DREAM BIG DREAMS ★

Date:

Before writing I was feeling_____

When writing, how do I want to feel?
1._____
2._____
3._____

What is my goal today for writing?
_____
_____

What did I do today to achieve my goal?
_____
_____

Writing Review Time: What worked and didn't work for me today?
_____
_____

★ DREAM BIG DREAMS ★

Date:

Before writing I was feeling_____

When writing, how do I want to feel?
1._____
2._____
3._____

What is my goal today for writing?
_____
_____

What did I do today to achieve my goal?
_____
_____

Writing Review Time: What worked and didn't work for me today?
_____
_____

★ DREAM BIG DREAMS ★

Date:

Before writing I was feeling_____

When writing, how do I want to feel?
1._____
2._____
3._____

What is my goal today for writing?
_____
_____

What did I do today to achieve my goal?
_____
_____

Writing Review Time: What worked and didn't work for me today?
_____
_____

★ DREAM BIG DREAMS ★

"We are not what we know but what we are willing to learn."
– Mary Catherine Bateson

Date:

Before writing I was feeling_____

When writing, how do I want to feel?
1._____
2._____
3._____

What is my goal today for writing?
_____
_____

What did I do today to achieve my goal?
_____
_____

Writing Review Time: What worked and didn't work for me today?
_____
_____

★ DREAM BIG DREAMS ★

Date:

Before writing I was feeling_____

When writing, how do I want to feel?
1._____
2._____
3._____

What is my goal today for writing?
_____
_____

What did I do today to achieve my goal?
_____
_____

Writing Review Time: What worked and didn't work for me today?
_____
_____

★ DREAM BIG DREAMS ★

Date:

Before writing I was feeling_____

When writing, how do I want to feel?
1._____
2._____
3._____

What is my goal today for writing?
_____
_____

What did I do today to achieve my goal?
_____
_____

Writing Review Time: What worked and didn't work for me today?
_____
_____

★ DREAM BIG DREAMS ★

Date:

Before writing I was feeling_____

When writing, how do I want to feel?
1._____
2._____
3._____

What is my goal today for writing?
_____
_____

What did I do today to achieve my goal?
_____
_____

Writing Review Time: What worked and didn't work for me today?
_____
_____

★ DREAM BIG DREAMS ★

Date:

Before writing I was feeling_____

When writing, how do I want to feel?
1._____
2._____
3._____

What is my goal today for writing?
_____
_____

What did I do today to achieve my goal?
_____
_____

Writing Review Time: What worked and didn't work for me today?
_____
_____

★ DREAM BIG DREAMS ★

Date:

Before writing I was feeling_____

When writing, how do I want to feel?
1._____
2._____
3._____

What is my goal today for writing?
_____
_____

What did I do today to achieve my goal?
_____
_____

Writing Review Time: What worked and didn't work for me today?
_____
_____

★ DREAM BIG DREAMS ★

Date:

Before writing I was feeling_____

When writing, how do I want to feel?
1._____
2._____
3._____

What is my goal today for writing?
_____
_____

What did I do today to achieve my goal?
_____
_____

Writing Review Time: What worked and didn't work for me today?
_____
_____

★ DREAM BIG DREAMS ★

"Somewhere, something incredible is waiting to be known."

– Carl Sagan

Date:

Before writing I was feeling_____

When writing, how do I want to feel?
1._____
2._____
3._____

What is my goal today for writing?
_____
_____

What did I do today to achieve my goal?
_____
_____

Writing Review Time: What worked and didn't work for me today?
_____
_____

★ DREAM BIG DREAMS ★

Date:

Before writing I was feeling_____

When writing, how do I want to feel?
1._____
2._____
3._____

What is my goal today for writing?
_____
_____

What did I do today to achieve my goal?
_____
_____

Writing Review Time: What worked and didn't work for me today?
_____
_____

★ DREAM BIG DREAMS ★

Date:

Before writing I was feeling_____

When writing, how do I want to feel?
1._____
2._____
3._____

What is my goal today for writing?
_____
_____

What did I do today to achieve my goal?
_____
_____

Writing Review Time: What worked and didn't work for me today?
_____
_____

★ DREAM BIG DREAMS ★

Date:

Before writing I was feeling_____

When writing, how do I want to feel?
1._____
2._____
3._____

What is my goal today for writing?
_____
_____

What did I do today to achieve my goal?
_____
_____

Writing Review Time: What worked and didn't work for me today?
_____
_____

★ DREAM BIG DREAMS ★

Date:

Before writing I was feeling_____

When writing, how do I want to feel?
1._____
2._____
3._____

What is my goal today for writing?
_____
_____

What did I do today to achieve my goal?
_____
_____

Writing Review Time: What worked and didn't work for me today?
_____
_____

★ DREAM BIG DREAMS ★

Date:

Before writing I was feeling_____

When writing, how do I want to feel?
1._____
2._____
3._____

What is my goal today for writing?
_____
_____

What did I do today to achieve my goal?
_____
_____

Writing Review Time: What worked and didn't work for me today?
_____
_____

★ DREAM BIG DREAMS ★

Date:

Before writing I was feeling_____

When writing, how do I want to feel?
1._____
2._____
3._____

What is my goal today for writing?
_____
_____

What did I do today to achieve my goal?
_____
_____

Writing Review Time: What worked and didn't work for me today?
_____
_____

★ DREAM BIG DREAMS ★

"The more that you read, the more things you will know.
The more that you learn the more places you'll go."
– Dr. Seuss

Date:

Before writing I was feeling_____

When writing, how do I want to feel?
1._____
2._____
3._____

What is my goal today for writing?
_____
_____

What did I do today to achieve my goal?
_____
_____

Writing Review Time: What worked and didn't work for me today?
_____
_____

★ DREAM BIG DREAMS ★

Date:

Before writing I was feeling_____

When writing, how do I want to feel?
1._____
2._____
3._____

What is my goal today for writing?
_____
_____

What did I do today to achieve my goal?
_____
_____

Writing Review Time: What worked and didn't work for me today?
_____
_____

★ DREAM BIG DREAMS ★

Date:

Before writing I was feeling_____

When writing, how do I want to feel?
1._____
2._____
3._____

What is my goal today for writing?
_____
_____

What did I do today to achieve my goal?
_____
_____

Writing Review Time: What worked and didn't work for me today?
_____
_____

★ DREAM BIG DREAMS ★

Date:

Before writing I was feeling_____

When writing, how do I want to feel?
1._____
2._____
3._____

What is my goal today for writing?
_____
_____

What did I do today to achieve my goal?
_____
_____

Writing Review Time: What worked and didn't work for me today?
_____
_____

★ DREAM BIG DREAMS ★

Date:

Before writing I was feeling_____

When writing, how do I want to feel?
1._____
2._____
3._____

What is my goal today for writing?
_____
_____

What did I do today to achieve my goal?
_____
_____

Writing Review Time: What worked and didn't work for me today?
_____
_____

★ DREAM BIG DREAMS ★

Date:

Before writing I was feeling_____

When writing, how do I want to feel?
1._____
2._____
3._____

What is my goal today for writing?
_____
_____

What did I do today to achieve my goal?
_____
_____

Writing Review Time: What worked and didn't work for me today?
_____
_____

★ DREAM BIG DREAMS ★

Date:

Before writing I was feeling_____

When writing, how do I want to feel?
1._____
2._____
3._____

What is my goal today for writing?
_____
_____

What did I do today to achieve my goal?
_____
_____

Writing Review Time: What worked and didn't work for me today?
_____
_____

★ DREAM BIG DREAMS ★

"The mind is not a vessel to be filled, but a fire to be kindled."

–Plutarch

Date:

Before writing I was feeling_____

When writing, how do I want to feel?
1._____
2._____
3._____

What is my goal today for writing?
_____
_____

What did I do today to achieve my goal?
_____
_____

Writing Review Time: What worked and didn't work for me today?
_____
_____

★ DREAM BIG DREAMS ★

Date:

Before writing I was feeling_____

When writing, how do I want to feel?
1._____
2._____
3._____

What is my goal today for writing?
_____
_____

What did I do today to achieve my goal?
_____
_____

Writing Review Time: What worked and didn't work for me today?
_____
_____

★ DREAM BIG DREAMS ★

Date:

Before writing I was feeling_____

When writing, how do I want to feel?
1._____
2._____
3._____

What is my goal today for writing?
_____
_____

What did I do today to achieve my goal?
_____
_____

Writing Review Time: What worked and didn't work for me today?
_____
_____

★ DREAM BIG DREAMS ★

Date:

Before writing I was feeling_____

When writing, how do I want to feel?
1._____
2._____
3._____

What is my goal today for writing?
_____
_____

What did I do today to achieve my goal?
_____
_____

Writing Review Time: What worked and didn't work for me today?
_____
_____

★ DREAM BIG DREAMS ★

Date:

Before writing I was feeling_____

When writing, how do I want to feel?
1._____
2._____
3._____

What is my goal today for writing?
_____
_____

What did I do today to achieve my goal?
_____
_____

Writing Review Time: What worked and didn't work for me today?
_____
_____

★ DREAM BIG DREAMS ★

Date:

Before writing I was feeling_____

When writing, how do I want to feel?
1._____
2._____
3._____

What is my goal today for writing?
_____
_____

What did I do today to achieve my goal?
_____
_____

Writing Review Time: What worked and didn't work for me today?
_____
_____

★ DREAM BIG DREAMS ★

Date:

Before writing I was feeling_____

When writing, how do I want to feel?
1._____
2._____
3._____

What is my goal today for writing?
_____
_____

What did I do today to achieve my goal?
_____
_____

Writing Review Time: What worked and didn't work for me today?
_____
_____

★ DREAM BIG DREAMS ★

"Even the smallest person can change the course of the future."
–J.R.R Tolkien

Date:

Before writing I was feeling_____

When writing, how do I want to feel?
1._____
2._____
3._____

What is my goal today for writing?
_____
_____

What did I do today to achieve my goal?
_____
_____

Writing Review Time: What worked and didn't work for me today?
_____
_____

★ DREAM BIG DREAMS ★

Date:

Before writing I was feeling_____

When writing, how do I want to feel?
1._____
2._____
3._____

What is my goal today for writing?
_____
_____

What did I do today to achieve my goal?
_____
_____

Writing Review Time: What worked and didn't work for me today?
_____
_____

★ DREAM BIG DREAMS ★

Date:

Before writing I was feeling_____

When writing, how do I want to feel?
1._____
2._____
3._____

What is my goal today for writing?
_____
_____

What did I do today to achieve my goal?
_____
_____

Writing Review Time: What worked and didn't work for me today?
_____
_____

★ DREAM BIG DREAMS ★

Date:

Before writing I was feeling_____

When writing, how do I want to feel?
1._____
2._____
3._____

What is my goal today for writing?
_____
_____

What did I do today to achieve my goal?
_____
_____

Writing Review Time: What worked and didn't work for me today?
_____
_____

★ DREAM BIG DREAMS ★

Date:

Before writing I was feeling_____

When writing, how do I want to feel?
1._____
2._____
3._____

What is my goal today for writing?
_____
_____

What did I do today to achieve my goal?
_____
_____

Writing Review Time: What worked and didn't work for me today?
_____
_____

★ DREAM BIG DREAMS ★

Date:

Before writing I was feeling_____

When writing, how do I want to feel?
1._____
2._____
3._____

What is my goal today for writing?
_____
_____

What did I do today to achieve my goal?
_____
_____

Writing Review Time: What worked and didn't work for me today?
_____
_____

★ DREAM BIG DREAMS ★

Date:

Before writing I was feeling_____

When writing, how do I want to feel?
1._____
2._____
3._____

What is my goal today for writing?
_____
_____

What did I do today to achieve my goal?
_____
_____

Writing Review Time: What worked and didn't work for me today?
_____
_____

★ DREAM BIG DREAMS ★

"Keep your eyes on the stars and your feet on the ground."

–Theodore Roosevelt

Review your achievements

★ DREAM BIG DREAMS ★

Review your achievements

★ DREAM BIG DREAMS ★

Review your achievements

★ DREAM BIG DREAMS ★

Review your achievements

★ DREAM BIG DREAMS ★

Printed in Great Britain
by Amazon